Robots

Contents

written by Jack Gabolinscy

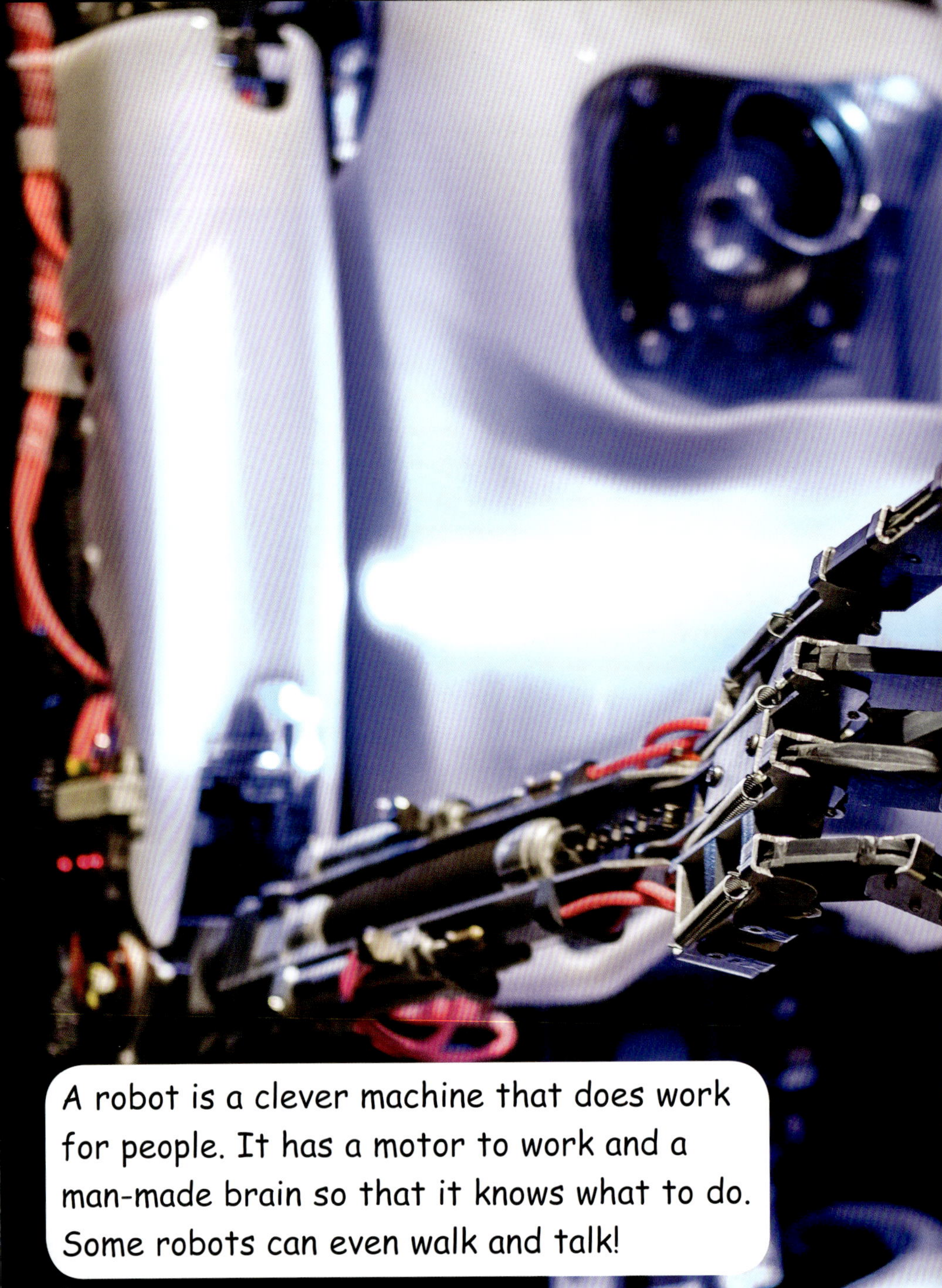

A robot is a clever machine that does work for people. It has a motor to work and a man-made brain so that it knows what to do. Some robots can even walk and talk!

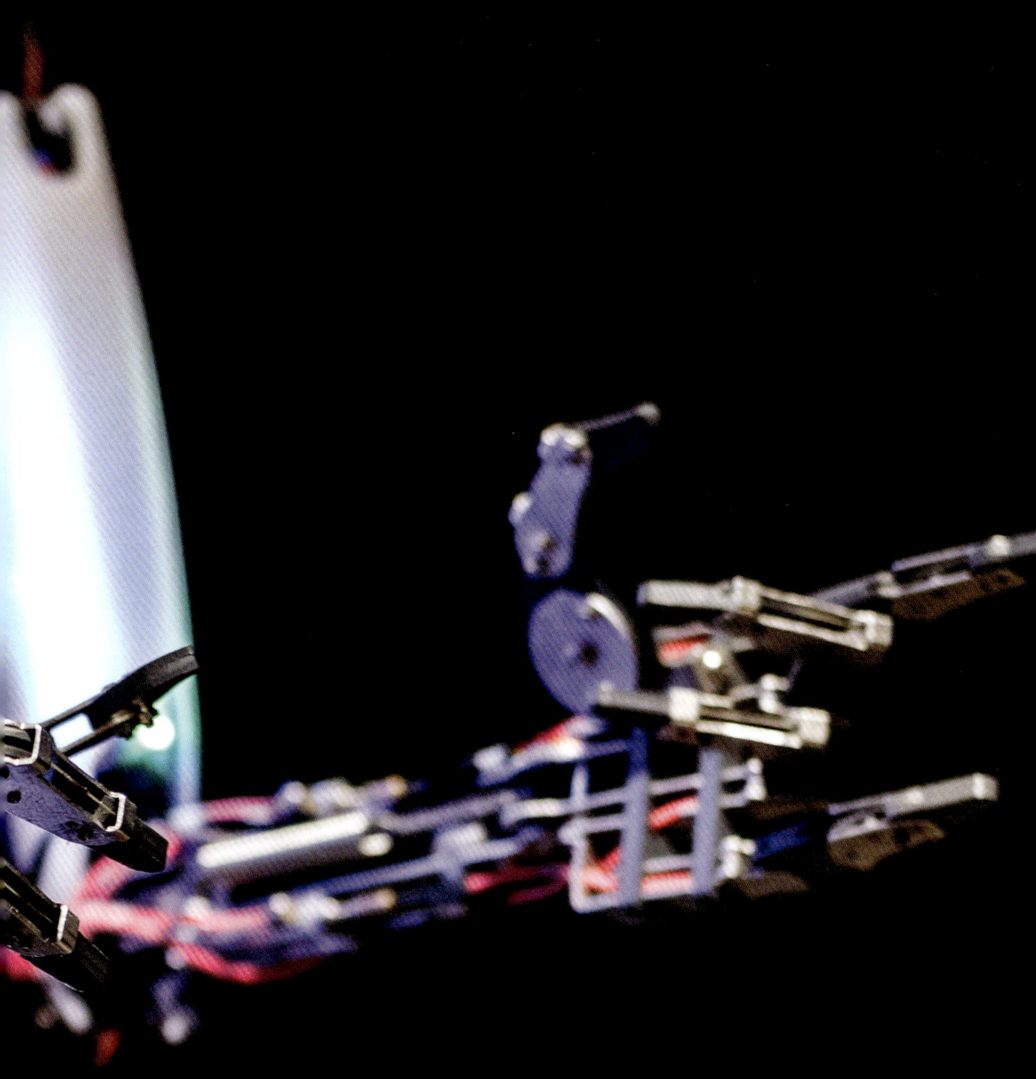

There are all kinds of robots. Some look
like animals, and some look like people.
There are robots that can fly or climb stairs.
Most robots are made to help people.

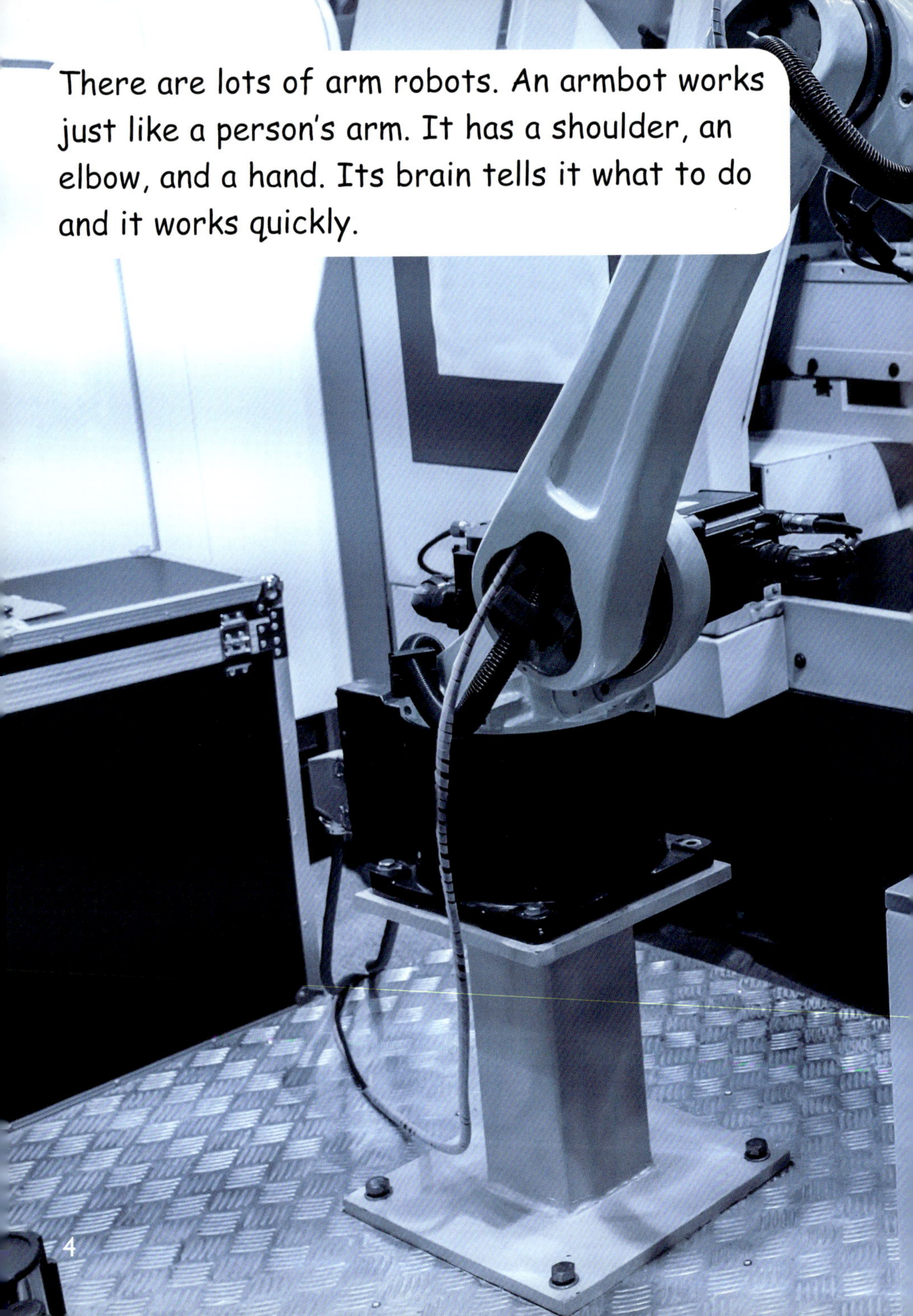

There are lots of arm robots. An armbot works just like a person's arm. It has a shoulder, an elbow, and a hand. Its brain tells it what to do and it works quickly.

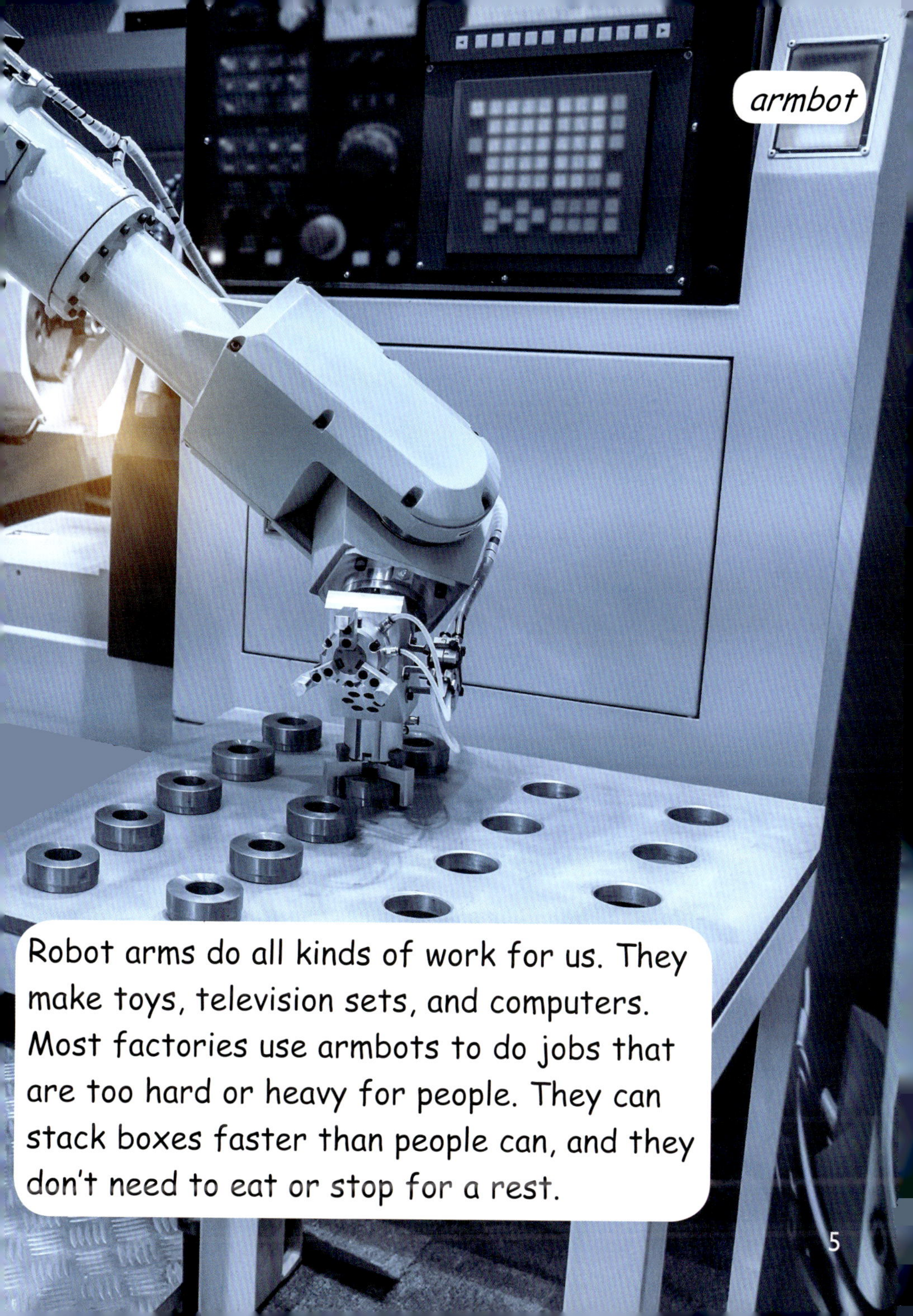

Robot arms do all kinds of work for us. They make toys, television sets, and computers. Most factories use armbots to do jobs that are too hard or heavy for people. They can stack boxes faster than people can, and they don't need to eat or stop for a rest.

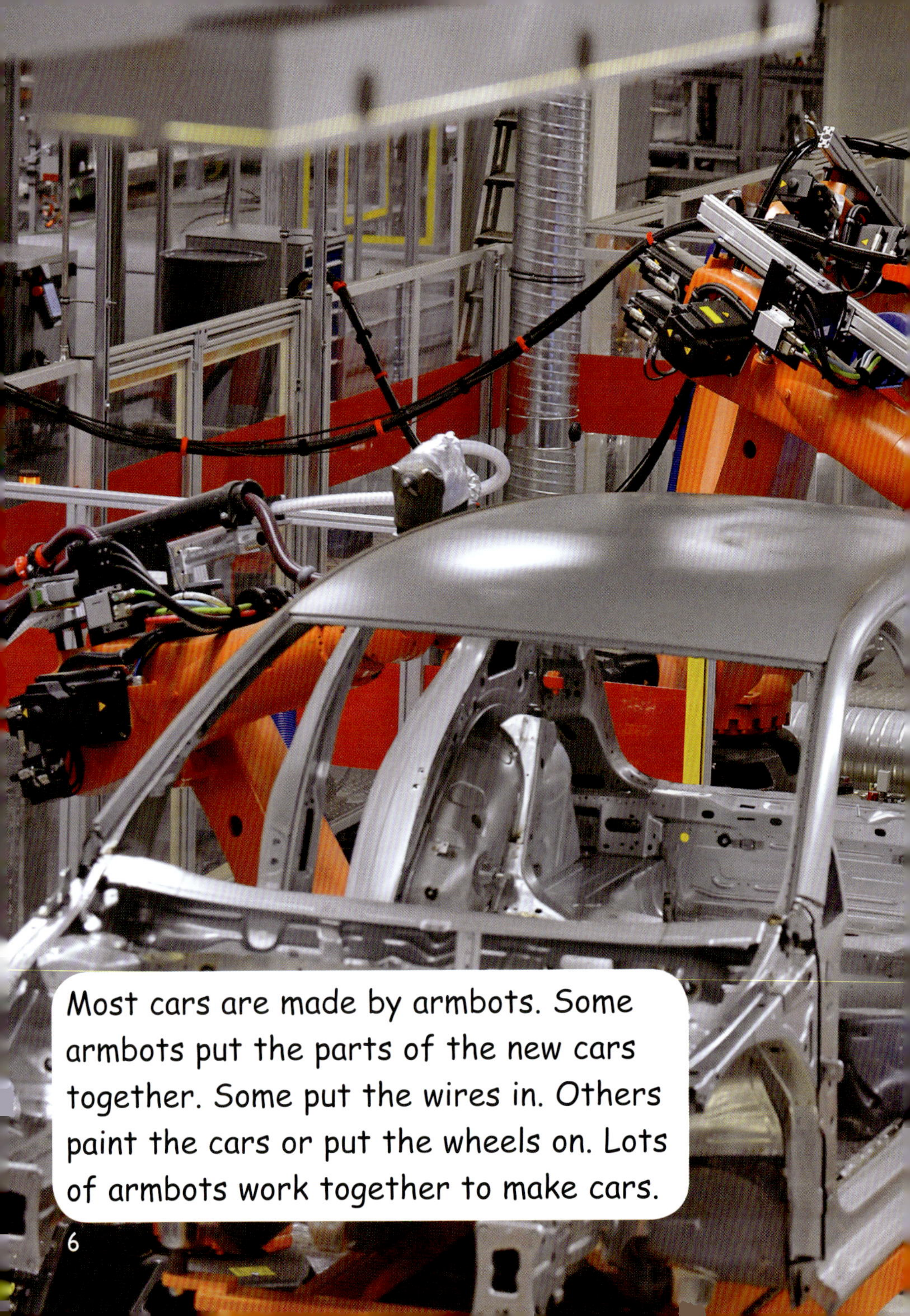

Most cars are made by armbots. Some armbots put the parts of the new cars together. Some put the wires in. Others paint the cars or put the wheels on. Lots of armbots work together to make cars.

Armbots do lots of other special jobs.
They help doctors do operations, and they
can be used to wash cars and planes.

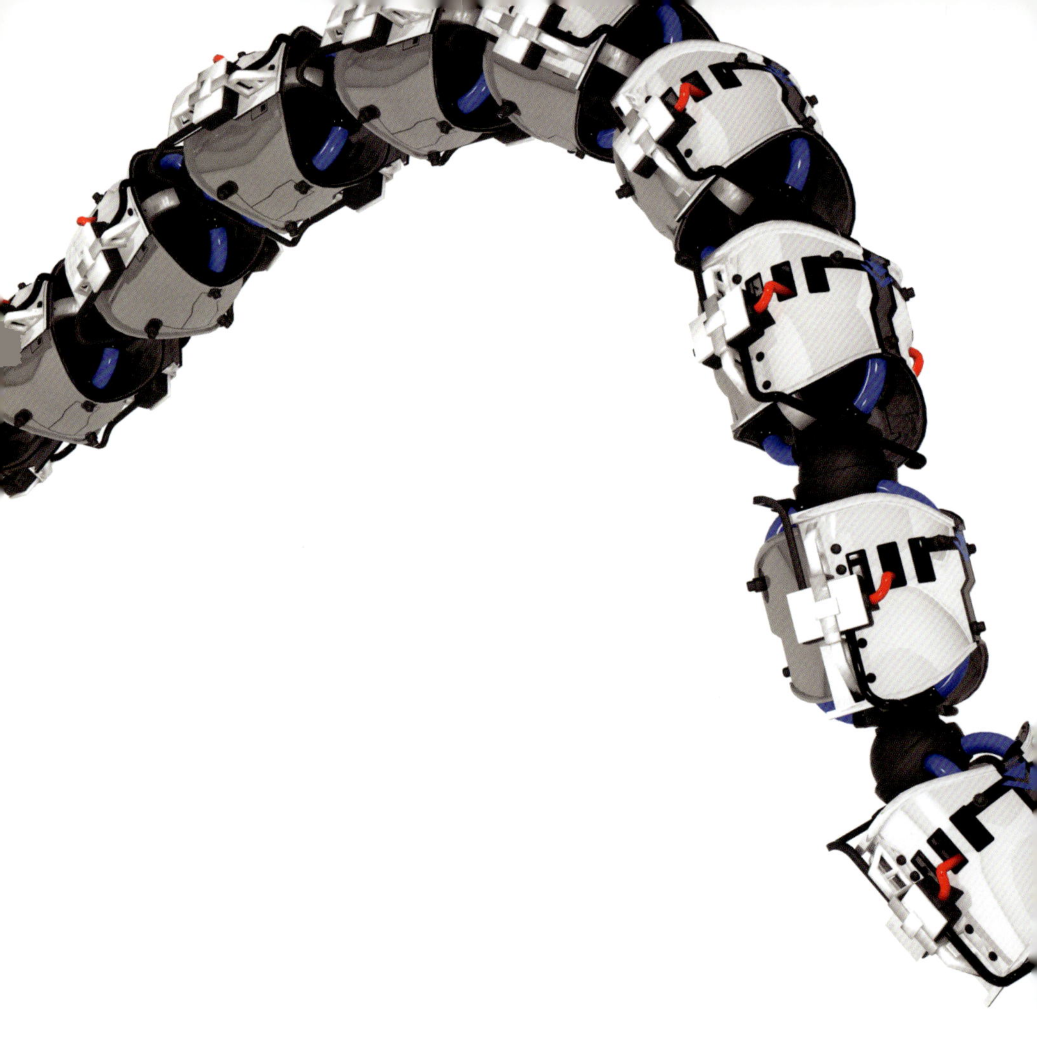

Some robots do dangerous work for us.
A snakebot is a long, thin robot. It can wiggle
and roll into small places where people can't go.

A snakebot can go into tunnels, into pipes, and under fallen-down buildings to look for trapped people. It has eyes and a camera. It takes pictures and sends them to a computer to help fix things or to rescue people.

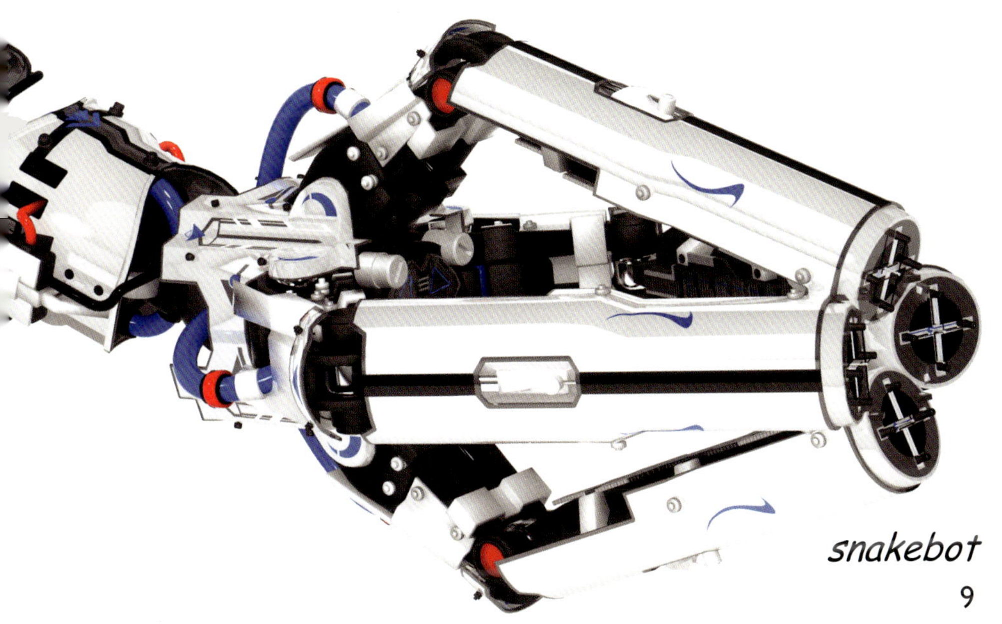

snakebot

There is a firefighting robot that can go
into a burning room to put out a fire.
It sees with a television eye and it squirts
foam onto the flames.

Robots can do other dangerous jobs like going underground into mines. They can go close to an erupting volcano or find ships that have sunk underwater.

There are robots to help people who can't see or walk. They can walk around in people's homes, down the street, and even go shopping. These robots have eyes and ears and feelers to tell them where they are going.

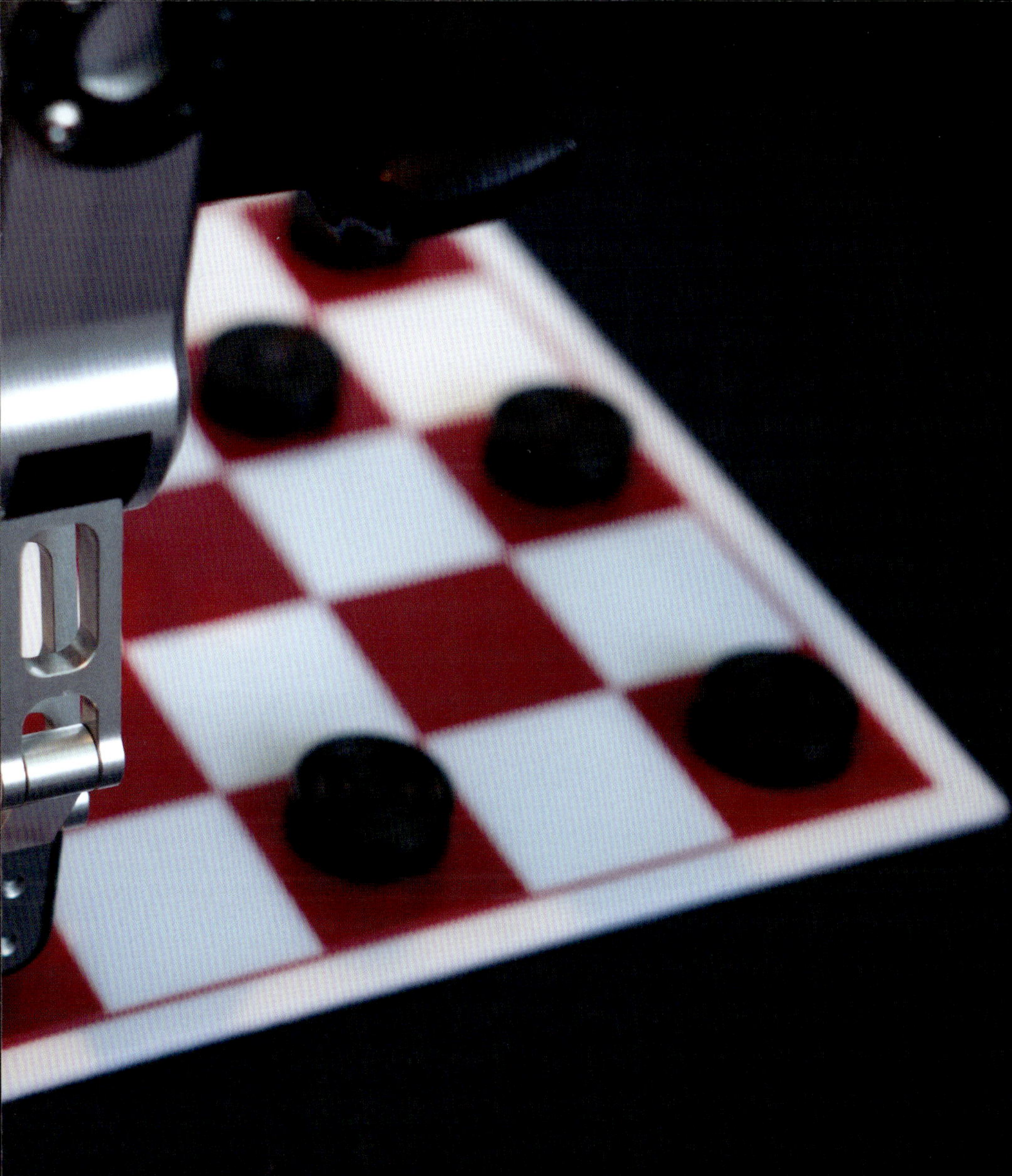

Some robots can play games like chess and soccer. They have batteries to give them energy, and clever fingers and eyes to see what they are doing.

Robots go into space to help astronauts with their work. Clever robots have been sent to explore the planet Mars because it is too far for people to go. They take photos to send back to Earth.

New robots are being made to help in more ways. There are robot arms and legs for disabled people. Firebots fight fires, spacebots fly into space, seabots go under the water, earthbots dig underground, and housebots do the housework.

In the future, there will be many new robots to do all kinds of work for us. One day you may see a robot at work and wonder if it is a robot or a real person.